EXTRAORDINARY SOLAR SYSTEM

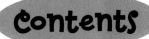

Contents

Space, the universe, or whatever you want to call it, is enormous! It's so big that it's almost impossible to imagine just how huge it is...and it goes on forever! Space is not empty — it contains loads of planets, moons, and stars! Our little corner of space is called the solar system. You can think of it as our neighborhood.

The Solar System

Our solar system is made up of the sun and everything that travels around it. The main objects that travel around the sun are the nine planets and their moons; huge chunks of rock and metal, called asteroids; and big, dirty icebergs, called comets. Our neighborhood is small in comparison with the whole universe, but it's busy!

Sun

Venus

Mercury

Mars

Neptune

The planets and the distances between them are not shown to scale.

Saturn

comet

Our planet Earth is the third nearest to the sun, but the distance between the two is still massive — a staggering 93 million miles (150 million km)!

hborhood

Pluto

Uranus

Earth

Jupiter

Asteroid belt — a band of asteroids that orbits the sun between Mars and Jupiter

EXTRA! EXTRA
Our sun is just one star in a never-ending universe of billions and billions of stars.

Feel the Force

The path of one object around another is called an orbit. Objects are kept in orbit by gravity — a strong pulling force that attracts objects toward one another. It's the same force that keeps your feet on the ground!

Lots of things are in orbit around Earth, for instance the moon, plus hundreds of satellites. These are small spacecraft that broadcast TV and telephone signals. There is also a manned space station, pieces of old rockets, and even lost astronaut gloves!

Wow!

The sizes of the objects in space are gigantic. It's hard to imagine just how big they are, but if the sun were the size of a grapefruit, the earth would only be as big as a pinhead!

Spaced Out!

People have studied the night sky since early times. Today, huge telescopes on mountains — and others high above the earth — search the universe. Machines called space probes are sent into space to send us photos of the other planets in our solar system.

EXTRA! EXTRA!
Not all space probes are successful! This Russian probe, called Phobos, was sent to study Mars in 1988, but its mission failed.

▲ The planets are too far away for astronauts to travel to (yet!) so scientists send space probes to study them instead. Probes fly close to planets and even land on them, then send back pictures.

Spying on Space

Astronomers are people who study the universe. They use telescopes to find out about space. Optical telescopes collect light from distant objects. The telescopes contain lenses and mirrors that make the objects look bigger. Radio telescopes collect radio waves given out by objects in space, and make pictures from them.

Gosh, it's noisy out there!

I spy with my little eye...

Hubble on High!

The Hubble Space Telescope was taken into orbit in 1990. Since then, it has taken many thousands of incredible pictures of the universe. Hubble is in space, way above the earth, so it can see faraway stars much more clearly than larger telescopes on the ground can.

Wow!

Until recently, ours was the only solar system that we knew existed. But planet-hunters using new telescopes and techniques have revealed that other stars have two or more planets orbiting them, too! These new planets may even be home to other life forms!

What

can I see in space?

You don't need a space probe to study the universe! On a clear night, you can use just your eyes to see the patterns of stars in the sky.

If you know where to look, you can see planets, too. When Venus is shining in the morning or the evening sky, it is easy to spot. It looks like a bright star.

With binoculars, you can see the colors of the stars better. You'll also be able to see the craters on the moon!

NEVER LOOK DIRECTLY AT THE SUN, OR YOU COULD DAMAGE YOUR EYES!

The Fiery Sun

Without the sun there would be no life on Earth — it's that simple. The sun is a huge star, which is a ball of superhot gases. It provides the heat, light, and energy that all living things need to live.

NEVER LOOK AT THE SUN!

Never look at the sun or at a solar eclipse with your naked eye or through binoculars or a telescope! It is so bright it will blind you!

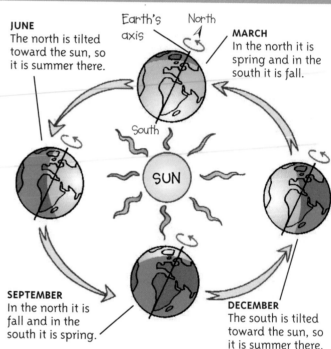

JUNE The north is tilted toward the sun, so it is summer there.

Earth's axis

North

MARCH In the north it is spring and in the south it is fall.

South

SUN

SEPTEMBER In the north it is fall and in the south it is spring.

DECEMBER The south is tilted toward the sun, so it is summer there.

Earth's axis
Day
SUN
Night
EARTH

Day and Night

Imagine an invisible rod that runs through the earth from the top to the bottom. This is its axis. Every 24 hours, the earth spins counterclockwise on its axis. As Earth turns, the side closer to the sun has warmth and light, or day. The side farther away from the sun is cold and dark, and here it is night.

Changing Seasons

As the earth spins on its axis, it also travels slowly around the sun, taking one whole year to complete the circuit. This journey makes the seasons. The earth's axis is tilted, so as it orbits the sun, different parts receive different levels of heat and light. When one part of Earth is tilted toward the sun, it is summer. When the same part is tilted away, it is winter. In between are spring and fall.

Disappearing Sun

1 MOON SUN
When the moon moves in front of the sun, the sun disappears from view for a short time. This is called a solar eclipse.

2 MOON
When the sun is totally covered, you can see stars in the sky and the corona — the beautiful silver-blue gases that surround the sun!

3 MOON
When the moon moves away again, sunlight bursts out in a brilliant flare. For a magical moment, the sun looks like a diamond ring!

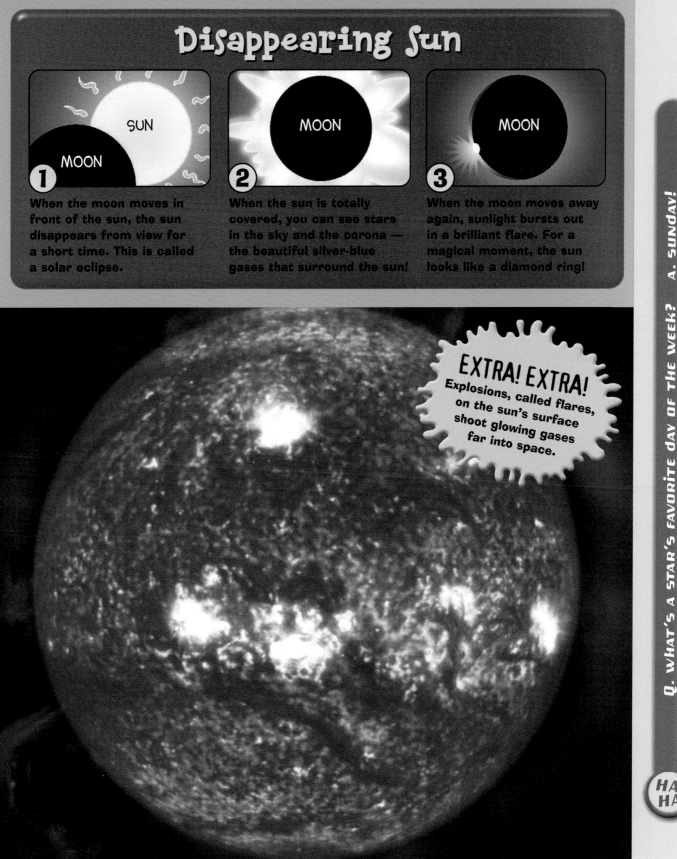

EXTRA! EXTRA!
Explosions, called flares, on the sun's surface shoot glowing gases far into space.

Q. WHAT'S A STAR'S FAVORITE DAY OF THE WEEK? A. SUNDAY!

HA HA

This satellite picture shows the fiery flames of the sun and the solar flares that leap out. All the stars in the sky are suns, too, seen as points of light because they are so distant.

Ouch! It's HOT

Mercury and Venus are the two planets closest to the sun. They can sometimes be seen shining in the sky before sunrise or after sunset. Venus is red-hot, and anyone who landed on it would die within minutes. You might survive on Mercury — but only if you land on its cold side.

Hot, but Cold

Mercury is the closest planet to the sun, so its sunny side is sizzling hot. It is also bare and rocky, and covered with craters — pits made when space rocks crashed into it. Some of its craters are so deep that sunlight never reaches their bottoms. Down there, it's dreadfully cold!

That's Weird!

It sounds impossible, but some astronomers think there might be ice on red-hot Mercury! Water could have frozen deep inside the dark craters, waiting to be used — maybe even drunk — by visiting astronauts in the future!

Fast-forward!

A planet's year is measured by the time it takes to orbit the sun. Mercury is so close to the sun that it whips around it in just 88 days! Can you imagine having a birthday once every 88 days? That's four birthdays each year!

Happy Birthday love from Sun

EXTRA! EXTRA!
Venus spins in the opposite direction from the other planets. That means if you could see the sun, it would rise in the west and set in the east!

Our best views of Venus came from the Magellan probe, which spent more than four years mapping the planet. It recorded weird, spiderlike ridges called arachnoids.

Nice weather we're having!

An Oven-hot Planet

All the planets, except Mercury, are surrounded by a layer of gases, called an atmosphere. Venus's atmosphere is made of poisonous clouds of burning acid, which are so thick that they almost block the sun's light. The clouds trap the sun's heat, like the glass in a greenhouse, making Venus's surface even hotter than Mercury's!

HA HA

9

Earth and Moon

Kept warm by the sun, Earth is a bright island in a cold, dark universe. With oceans full of water, lush forests, and breathable air, it is unique in the solar system! But on the moon, it's a different story.

Looking Back at Home

Imagine you are an astronaut, floating outside a space station....Take a look at the amazing view of Earth! From space, it looks like a beautiful blue-green marble, with white swirling clouds. You can see orange deserts, snowcapped mountains, and magnificent blue oceans beneath you. And at night, towns and cities shine like stars!

Hi, Mom!

The Birth of the Moon!

1 Most astronomers believe the moon was once part of the earth. Millions of years ago, a huge piece of space rock smashed into our planet.

2 The crash was enormous. The huge space rock shattered and all the bits from the collision were flung into orbit around the earth.

3 Over a long period of time, due to the pulling force of gravity, the shattered pieces all clumped together to form the moon. Wow!

Walking on the Moon

In 1969, when the first man stepped onto the moon, the whole world celebrated! It was a great scientific achievement. During the *Apollo* missions to the moon, astronauts took photos, did experiments, and studied the moonscape in detail. The astronauts' footprints are lasting evidence of this feat. There's no wind or rain on the moon to wash them away!

EXTRA! EXTRA!
There is less gravity on the moon than on Earth, which means the astronauts didn't feel so heavy. They found it easier to hop like a kangaroo than to walk!

This astronaut is Harrison Schmitt, a rock specialist from the *Apollo 17* mission. The priceless rocks that the astronauts collected are still being studied today.

Mighty Mars!

Scientists and writers of books and films have been fascinated for centuries by Mars and Martians! Even though Earth won't really be invaded by Martians, life may exist under the surface of Mars, or even inside its red rocks!

Confusing Canals

Long ago, people believed that Mars had canals, or channels, cut by Martians for carrying water to their cities! Of course, there are no cities on Mars, but it does have hundreds of channels. These are the remains of rivers from when Mars was a warmer, wetter world.

Wow!

Mars is only half the size of Earth, but it has a huge landmark on its surface! Olympus Mons is the biggest volcano in the solar system. It is so high — 15 miles (24 km) — that it makes Mount Everest, Earth's tallest mountain, look like a molehill!

You don't impress ME!

This photo shows Mars's surface. The robot Sojourner, from the Pathfinder space probe, examines a large rock.

How

do we know about Mars?

In 1997, the Pathfinder probe visited Mars. It landed in the Ares Valley, bouncing on big air bags to protect the probe.

Pathfinder recorded the weather and photographed the strange landscape, while its robot rover, Sojourner, studied the rocks up close.

GREETINGS FROM MARS!

More recently, the Mars Global Surveyor probe has sent back huge amounts of new information, including pictures showing that Mars may once have had lakes!

Gas Giants

The planets that lie beyond Mars are nothing like those that are closer to the sun. Jupiter and Saturn are gas giants — bloated balls of gas and liquid with deep, stormy, swirling atmospheres. These planets are ringed by icy pieces of dust and rock and dozens of unusual moons!

Monster Planet

Jupiter is by far the largest planet in our solar system. It is a dozen times wider than Earth! It is marked with colorful bands of gases and you can see it, like a star, with the naked eye.

Ugh — It's a Spot!

Jupiter's cloudy surface is covered in huge storms. One of them is the biggest in the whole solar system! The Great Red Spot is a terrifying hurricane almost three times the size of Earth! Its fierce winds whip across the planet at over 250 miles per hour (400 kmh).

Stormy weather ahead!

EXTRA! EXTRA!
A spacecraft could never land on Jupiter because it does not have a solid surface. The doomed craft would just sink into the gas!

Prize Rings

Saturn used to be called the Ringed Planet — until scientists discovered other planets had rings, too! But Saturn's rings are still the biggest. They look like solid hoops, but they are actually made of countless millions of chunks of rock and ice. If you were a good space pilot, you could fly through them!

Moon-hunting Fever

Scientists used to think Jupiter and Saturn had only a dozen or so moons each. But pictures taken recently by space probes and telescopes have revealed many more moons. And more and more are being discovered each month! As this book was being written, Jupiter had 28 moons and Saturn 30...but that might have changed by the time you read this page!

That's Weird!

Saturn looks pretty big and solid, doesn't it? But in fact, it's not solid at all. The gases that make up Saturn are so light that if you could find a bathtub big enough, Saturn would actually float in the water!

Far-flying

At the edge of the solar system, where it is unbelievably cold and dark, Uranus, Neptune, and Pluto take many years to orbit the sun.

EXTRA! EXTRA!
Neptune has rings around its center. They're thicker in some places than in others and are probably the remains of a smashed-up moon!

HA HA

Several dark spots that may be fierce storms have been seen on Neptune's surface. The largest, called the Great Dark Spot, is so gigantic, it's about the same size as Earth!

Planets

Pretty Planets

Uranus and Neptune are so far away that you can only just see them with the naked eye, as faint stars. If you could get closer, you'd find that they are both, in fact, about four times wider than Earth! Uranus looks like a huge ball of smoky-green gas, while Neptune looks blue. This is because the gases in their atmospheres reflect blue and green light.

Hey, that color really suits you!

Thanks! You, too.

That's Weird!

Uranus is unique in the way it spins. The other planets rotate upright, like spinning tops, but Uranus rolls around the sun on its side, like a barrel. Astronomers think it was hit so hard by a comet in its past that it was pushed over like a bowling pin!

OOF!

Moons Galore

Like Jupiter and Saturn, Uranus and Neptune have many moons. Neptune has only eight, but Uranus has at least 21! Long ago, Uranus's moon Miranda may have been smashed into pieces, then re-formed. Triton, Neptune's largest moon, has hot springs called geysers on its pink, icy surface!

Living on the Edge

Icy Pluto is the only planet that hasn't been explored by a space probe yet, but telescopes have revealed a few of its secrets. It is the smallest planet of all, just 1,413 miles (2,274 km) across. It's so tiny that some astronomers question whether it is a planet at all! Its only moon, called Charon, is nearly half as big as Pluto itself and orbits very close to it.

Heading Your Way

When you gaze up at night, space might look peaceful — but it isn't! There are thousands of space rocks zipping around in all directions. Most are pieces of dust and grit, but others are bigger chunks that may land on Earth.

Big Bash!

Pieces of space rock that fall to Earth are called meteorites. This one is lit up to show crystals inside it. Meteorites can be enormous. Around 50,000 years ago, a massive one smacked into the Arizona desert. It blasted out a huge crater — a hole 570 feet (175 m) deep and 4,000 feet (1,220 m) wide.

Space Fireworks

When pieces of space rock are flying through space, they are called meteoroids. As they enter Earth's atmosphere, they make bright streaks in the sky, called meteors or shooting stars. At certain times of the year, you can see hundreds appear in a few hours. When this happens, it is called a meteor shower.

Killer Rock!

Waazzaat??

1

Sixty-five million years ago, dinosaurs ruled the earth... so why did they die? Scientists think a big space rock hit Earth, causing a fire that threw smoke into the sky.

So long, Earth....

2

The sun was blotted out by the smoke. There was no sunlight, so the plants died and Earth became unbearably cold. The dinosaurs died from lack of warmth and food.

18

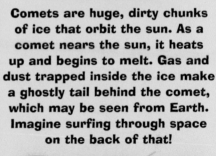

Wow!

Comets are huge, dirty chunks of ice that orbit the sun. As a comet nears the sun, it heats up and begins to melt. Gas and dust trapped inside the ice make a ghostly tail behind the comet, which may be seen from Earth. Imagine surfing through space on the back of that!

This is the comet Hale-Bopp, which appeared in Earth's skies in 1997. It was one of the most visible and beautiful comets to appear during the 20th century.

Star Babies

Let's look outside the solar system at all the other stars! On a clear night, you can see several thousand stars, but there are billions more. New stars are born each day in clouds of gas and dust called nebulae.

Connect the Dots

Stars are scattered across the sky, but over many years, people have connected them into patterns, called constellations. In the night sky, there are shapes that represent a lion, a bear, and even a dragon! Before hi-tech navigation systems were invented, sailors voyaged across the oceans using the stars as their guide.

Turn left at the Big Dipper!

Jewel Box in the Sky

The sun is a single star, but most stars in the universe are seen in pairs, or threes, or even larger groups, called clusters. Some of these clusters, such as the Pleiades (above), are made of dozens of stars, but others contain up to one million twinkling stars!

Wow!

If you could fly away from the sun in a spaceship, you would see that it is just one star in a cloud of millions. Eventually, if you traveled even further away, you would see that the sun is part of a huge collection of stars — a galaxy. Our galaxy is called the Milky Way. There are billions of other galaxies in the universe, too!

I'm the Milky Way! X marks the spot for the solar system!

EXTRA! EXTRA!
The amazing clouds in this photo are columns of dust and gas in the Eagle nebula. If you could travel at the speed of light, it would take you 7,000 years to get there!

▲ In a nebula, small, thick parts clump together into a ball. The ball becomes smaller and hotter and a new star is born. It begins to shine brilliantly, like our sun.

Brain Benders

Scientists are making exciting discoveries about the solar system and the universe all the time. Each discovery leads to amazing theories. So put your brain in gear and find out what awesome ideas astronomers are coming up with!

Space Patrol!

Many astronomers think that at some time in the future, we may be hit by a massive asteroid or comet — and end up as dead as the dinosaurs! Scientists don't know if or when this will happen, though. They spend their time tracking these moving missiles, in the hope that they might be able to deflect or destroy them long before they reach their target!

Big Bangs...and Crunches!

1 Most astronomers think the universe was born in a huge explosion, known as the Big Bang, around 13 billion years ago! Since then, the universe has been growing bigger and bigger and bigger!

2 The tiny bits that make up everything in the universe are known as matter. Astronomers try to determine how much matter there is in space, so they can figure out what might happen in the future.

3 One theory says that billions of years in the future, the universe will stop expanding and start to collapse on itself. Eventually, all matter will crash together in a devastating Big Crunch!

Internet Astronomer

With the help of a computer — and an adult's permission — you can become an astronomer and work out your own mind-bending theories! There are many programs and Web sites that recreate the night sky on your screen. You can even become a time traveler in space and find out how the sky looked centuries ago or how it will appear in the future!

EXTRA! EXTRA!

New research suggests that every galaxy, including our own, has a huge black hole at its center, hungrily devouring gas and dust — and even whole stars!

Q. WHAT KIND OF POEM CAN YOU FIND IN OUTER SPACE?   A. A UNI-VERSE!

A black hole can be formed from the remains of a dead star. It has such strong gravity that even light is sucked in. This is an idea of how a black hole might look!

Is Anyone Out There?

Have aliens visited Earth? Many people think so! They claim that they have seen alien spacecraft called UFOs, or Unidentified Flying Objects, zooming through the sky and even on Earth!

Buzzed by Aliens?

UFOs have been reported all over the world and sometimes photographed. Scientists insist they are all either mistakes or deliberate fakes. Many astronomers believe that there are intelligent aliens in space, who might be sending radio signals to us. So SETI, the Search for Extra Terrestrial Intelligence, uses radio telescopes to listen for alien messages. They haven't heard anything yet!

Can you repeat that, please?

Mfbkj nsjn? [Translation: Can you repeat that, please?]

In 1984, a meteorite from Mars was found. Then, in 1996, scientists became very excited when microscopes showed strange shapes inside the meteorite. Some scientists think these may be tiny preserved life forms! But the debate is still raging.

Oh, no, it isn't!

Oh, yes, it is!

This faked photo of UFOs over Florida shows a popular image of alien spacecraft — flying saucers!

Where

might life exist in space?

Let me out!

Simple life forms might exist wherever there is water. A few scientists think water still exists on Mars, in warm spots beneath the surface.

Brrr! It's icy in here!

It is possible that water, and even life forms, may exist under the icy crusts of Jupiter's moons Europa and Ganymede.

Uh-oh!

Life might also lurk below the thick orange clouds of Saturn's moon Titan. Life might lie in pools or even oceans of tar-like material!

The Year 2025

Futuristic movies show us that in the future we will travel to distant stars, where we will fight alien monsters and discover strange civilizations. Maybe. But in the next few decades, it's more likely that we will revisit the moon, and even land on Mars!

Inside the ISS

Seventeen different countries are working together to build an International Space Station (ISS) high above the earth! When it is finished, astronauts will use the craft as an orbiting laboratory. They will carry out experiments, make things, such as new medicines, and study the earth and space. By 2007, the ISS may be big enough for six astronauts to live and work inside.

Back to the Moon

1 Hi, honey, I'm home!

Many scientists want to send people back to the moon, but this time to live there! A moon base might look like lots of huge tin cans joined by tunnels, or it might even be built underground!

2 Hurry up. I'm thirsty.

Astronauts living on the moon would explore its surface, looking for ice, which can be turned into water. They would also test space equipment and build powerful telescopes, too!

EXTRA! EXTRA!

By the year 2025, astronauts may have landed on Mars. But the planet is so far away that it will take six months to get there!

Wow!

It's true! In 10 years you may be able to go on vacation in space! Travel companies have plans to build space hotels in orbit, where people can vacation looking down at the earth! But it would be expensive — tens of thousands of dollars a day!

The first base on Mars might look something like this. Astronauts will live here for a whole year. To survive, they will grow their own food and make their own water, fuel, and air.

Q. WHAT IS AN ASTRONAUT'S FAVORITE MEAL?   A. LAUNCH!

HA HA

Extra Amazing

Want to know the nitty-gritty? Here are a few facts and figures to amaze your brain. Don't forget, you can see a lot of what's out in the solar system just by looking at the clear night sky.

SUN

MERCURY

VENUS

EARTH

MARS

The planets are not shown to scale. Find out below their diameters (how wide they are) and the distances between them and the sun.

JUPITER

Sky Watching

Want to watch the night sky? Here are some top tips. Observe the sky from a place that isn't spoiled by artificial light. If you're observing from somewhere away from home, make sure an adult goes with you. Dress warmly — if you're standing still, you'll get cold late at night, even in summer!

Planet Facts

MERCURY
Diameter:
3,032miles
(4,880 km)
Distance from Sun:
36 million miles (58 million km)
Moons:
None

VENUS
Diameter:
7,521 miles
(12,104 km)
Distance from Sun:
67 million miles
(108 million km)
Moons:
None

EARTH
Diameter:
7,927 miles
(12,756 km)
Distance from Sun:
93 million miles
(150 million km)
Moons:
1

MARS
Diameter:
4,222 miles
(6,794 km)
Distance from Sun:
142 million miles
(228 million km)
Moons:
2

JUPITER
Diameter:
88,850 miles
(142,984 km)
Distance from Sun:
483 million miles
(778 million km)
Moons:
28

What a Whopper!

The biggest meteorite ever to be found on Earth landed in Namibia, Africa. It was estimated to weigh a whopping 60 tons — as heavy as 12 elephants!

See a Shower!

Meteor showers happen at the same time every year. They are visible for a few days on either side of the peak dates below. Don't worry about which way to look. Just find a dark site and watch the sky. You'll soon figure out where they're coming from.

- the Quadrantids, January 4: typically blue, bright, with long glowing trails
- the Perseids, August 12: very rich shower, blue-white, fast-moving meteors
- the Orionids, October 22: very fast with fine trails
- the Leonids, November 17: every 33 years this shower becomes a storm, and the sky fills with shooting stars for a short time
- the Geminids, December 13: rich, colorful shower

Rock Monster

The biggest asteroid spotted in the asteroid belt so far is called Ceres. It was discovered in 1801 by a Sicilian monk, called Guiseppe Piazzi. It's an amazing 580 miles (933 km) wide!

Good heavens!

SATURN

URANUS

NEPTUNE

SATURN	URANUS	NEPTUNE	PLUTO
Diameter: 74,901 miles (120,536 km)	**Diameter:** 31,765 miles (51,118 km)	**Diameter:** 30,779 miles (49,532 km)	**Diameter:** 1,413 miles (2,274 km)
Distance from Sun: 887 million miles (1,427 million km)	**Distance from Sun:** 1,784 million miles (2,871 million km)	**Distance from Sun:** 2,796 million miles (4,500 million km)	**Distance from Sun:** 3,674 million miles (5,913 million km)
Moons: 30	**Moons:** 21	**Moons:** 8	**Moons:** 1

PLUTO and its moon CHARON

True or False?

How much do you really know about the solar system? To find out, test yourself with these true or false questions. Answers are on page 32, but no cheating!

1 Saturn has 542 moons.

2 The band of rocks between Mars and Jupiter is called the asteroid belt.

3 The Hubble Space Telescope was launched in 1822.

4 The planet in this picture is called Earth.

Who do you think I am?

5 The earth is bigger than the sun.

6 Mercury's year is 88 days long.

7 Robots have explored the surface of Mars.

Space Terms

asteroid
A large rocky and/or metallic object that travels around the sun like a small planet. A band of asteroids, called the asteroid belt, orbits the sun between Mars and Jupiter.

astronomer
A scientist who studies stars and planets.

atmosphere
The layer of gases that surrounds a planet.

Big Bang
An enormous explosion that many astronomers think caused the birth of the universe.

comet
A huge chunk of dirty ice that orbits the sun.

day
The time a planet takes to spin once on its axis.

galaxy
A huge group of many thousands of millions of stars. Our galaxy is called the Milky Way.

meteoroid
A small piece of dust or rock that orbits the sun. The bright streak it makes as it enters the earth's atmosphere is called a meteor, or shooting star. If a meteoroid hits Earth, it is called a meteorite.

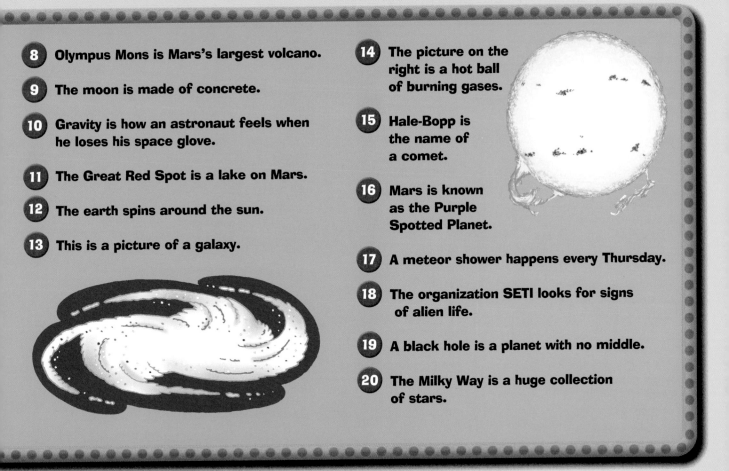

8. Olympus Mons is Mars's largest volcano.

9. The moon is made of concrete.

10. Gravity is how an astronaut feels when he loses his space glove.

11. The Great Red Spot is a lake on Mars.

12. The earth spins around the sun.

13. This is a picture of a galaxy.

14. The picture on the right is a hot ball of burning gases.

15. Hale-Bopp is the name of a comet.

16. Mars is known as the Purple Spotted Planet.

17. A meteor shower happens every Thursday.

18. The organization SETI looks for signs of alien life.

19. A black hole is a planet with no middle.

20. The Milky Way is a huge collection of stars.

Milky Way
The name given to the spiral-shaped galaxy in which Earth and the solar system lie.

moon
A natural object that orbits a planet.

orbit
The path of one object around another, such as a moon around a planet.

planet
A large spherical object, made of rock and/or gases and liquid, that orbits a star.

satellite
An object that orbits another one. Artificial satellites are small spacecraft that collect information and broadcast TV and radio signals.

solar system
The sun, the nine planets, and all the thousands of asteroids and comets that go around the sun.

space probe
A machine carrying scientific instruments, which is sent from Earth to study a planet, moon, comet, or asteroid.

star
A ball of flaming gases. The sun is a star.

sun
The star nearest to the earth. The sun is at the center of our solar system.

year
The length of time it takes for a planet to make one full trip around its star.

Index

Answers

1 False	11 False
2 True	12 True
3 False	13 True
4 False	14 True
5 False	15 True
6 True	16 False
7 True	17 False
8 True	18 True
9 False	19 False
10 False	20 True

Author: Stuart Atkinson
Illustrations: Andrew Peters; pp. 2-3, 27 Julian Baum;
pp. 12, 14, 15, 17, 28-29 Sebastian Quigley
Consultant: Sue Becklake, BSc
Photographs: Cover: Lynette Cook/Science Photo
Library; p. 4 Astrofoto/Bruce Coleman; p. 7 NASA/
Science Photo Library; p. 8 NASA/Science Photo Library;
p. 9 NASA/Science Photo Library; p. 11 top NASA/
Science Photo Library; p. 11 bottom NASA/Science Photo
Library; pp. 12-13 NASA/Science Photo Library;
p. 16 Astrofoto/Bruce Coleman; p. 18 Detlev van
Ravenswaay/Science Photo Library; p. 19 Astrofoto/Bruce
Coleman; p. 20 Tony & Daphne Hallas/Science Photo
Library; p. 21 NHPA/Tom and Therisa Stack; p. 23
Mehau Kulyk/Science Photo Library; pp. 24-25
Astrofoto/Bruce Coleman; p. 26 NASA.

Created by act-two for Scholastic Inc. Copyright © act-two, 2001
All rights reserved. Published by Scholastic Inc.

ISBN 0-439-28605-0

19 18 17 16 15 14 13   6/0

Printed in the U.S.A.

First Scholastic printing, October 2001